T0395668

HEROES OF AMERICAN HISTORY
AMELIA EARHART

CONTENTS

- 2 Interactive eBook Code
- 4 Who Was Amelia Earhart?
- 6 Growing Up
- 8 Overcoming Obstacles
- 10 Values
- 12 Aviation
- 14 Thoughts from Amelia
- 16 Pilot
- 18 Achievements and Successes
- 20 Amelia Earhart Timeline
- 22 Cause and Effect
- 24 Sight Words

Amelia Earhart

Who Was Amelia Earhart?

Amelia Earhart was a famous U.S. pilot. She was the first woman to fly across the Atlantic Ocean.

Amelia flew 14,000 feet (4,267 meters) high in an airplane, higher than any woman had flown before.

Amelia Earhart 5

6   Heroes of American History

Growing Up

Amelia was born in Atchison, Kansas. Her family moved around often. Amelia also lived in Iowa and Illinois.

Today, Atchison is home to the Amelia Earhart Birthplace Museum.

Atchison

KANSAS

Overcoming Obstacles

In the 1930s, most of the people who flew airplanes were men. Amelia showed the world that women could fly airplanes, too.

Amelia Earhart 9

10 Heroes of American History

Amelia Earhart 13

14   Heroes of American History

Thoughts from Amelia

Amelia believed that all women should follow their dreams. She encouraged them to excel.

"There's more to life than being a passenger."
– Amelia Earhart

Pilot

Amelia earned her pilot's license in 1923. She set many flying records.

Amelia was the first woman to fly across the United States.

Values

Amelia was brave and adventurous. Flying could be dangerous. She wanted to do it anyway.

Amelia Earhart

Aviation

Amelia was interested in aviation. She started a group called the Ninety-Nines. This group helped women become pilots.

12   Heroes of American History

HEROES OF AMERICAN HISTORY

AMELIA EARHART

Lily Erlic

openlightbox.com

LIGHTBOX

Go to
www.openlightbox.com
and enter this book's unique code.

ACCESS CODE
LBXN9424

Lightbox is an all-inclusive digital solution for the teaching and learning of curriculum topics in an original, groundbreaking way.

OPTIMIZED FOR
- ✓ TABLETS
- ✓ SMART BOARDS
- ✓ COMPUTERS
- ✓ AND MUCH MORE!

STANDARD FEATURES OF LIGHTBOX

- **AUDIO** High-quality narration using text-to-speech system
- **VIDEOS** Embedded high-definition video clips
- **ACTIVITIES** Printable PDFs that can be emailed and graded
- **WEBLINKS** Curated links to external, child-safe resources
- **SLIDESHOWS** Pictorial overviews of key concepts
- **INTERACTIVE MAPS** Interactive maps and aerial satellite imagery
- **QUIZZES** Ten multiple choice questions that are automatically graded and emailed for teacher assessment
- **KEY WORDS** Matching key concepts to their definitions

SUPPLEMENTARY RESOURCES

- **SHARE** Share titles within your Learning Management System (LMS) or Library Circulation System
- **CURRICULUM** Find national and state curriculum correlations
- **CITATION** Create bibliographical references following APA, CMSO, and MLA styles

VIDEOS

WEBLINKS

SLIDESHOWS

QUIZZES

This title is part of our Lightbox digital subscription

1-Year Texas Subscription
978-1-5105-8659-8

Access hundreds of Lightbox titles with our digital subscription.
Sign up for a **FREE** subscription trial at **www.openlightbox.com/trial**

The digital components of this book are guaranteed to stay active for at least five years from the date of publication.

Amelia Earhart   17

18 Heroes of American History

Achievements and Successes

Amelia was the first woman to try to fly around the world. She and her airplane disappeared during this flight.

The Smithsonian National Air and Space Museum, in Washington, DC, has some of Amelia's airplanes in its collection.

Amelia Earhart

Amelia Earhart Timeline

1897 Born

1922 Flies 14,000 feet high

1928 Flies across the Atlantic Ocean

1921 Buys her first airplane

20 Heroes of American History

1935 Flies from Hawaii to California

1997 Some researchers believe Amelia's bones are found.

1937 Lost at sea

2025 Scientist Richard Pettigrew organizes a new search for Amelia's airplane.

Amelia Earhart   21

Cause and Effect

22 Heroes of American History

Cause
Amelia took flying lessons.

↓

Effect
She earned her pilot's license.

Cause
Amelia was a good pilot.

↓

Effect
She set many flying records.

Amelia Earhart 23

SIGHT WORDS

Research has shown that as much as 65 percent of all written material published in English is made up of 300 words. These 300 words cannot be taught using pictures or learned by sounding them out. They must be recognized by sight. This book contains 58 common sight words to help young readers improve their reading fluency and comprehension. This book also teaches young readers several important content words, such as proper nouns. These words are paired with pictures to aid in learning and improve understanding.

Page	Sight Words First Appearance
4	a, an, any, before, feet, first, had, high, in, she, than, the, to, was, who
7	also, and, around, family, her, home, is, often, up
8	could, men, most, of, people, that, too, were, world
11	be, do, it
12	group, started, this
15	all, being, follow, from, life, more, should, their, them, there, thoughts
16	many, set, states
19	air, has, its, some, try

Page	Content Words First Appearance
4	airplane, Amelia Earhart, Atlantic Ocean, pilot, woman
7	Amelia Earhart Birthplace Museum, Atchison, Illinois, Iowa, Kansas
8	obstacles
11	values
12	aviation, Ninety-Nines
14	dreams, passenger
16	license, records, United States
19	achievements, collection, flight, Smithsonian National Air and Space Museum, successes, Washington, DC

Published by Lightbox Learning Inc.
276 5th Avenue, Suite 704 #917
New York, NY 10001
Website: www.openlightbox.com

Copyright ©2026 Lightbox Learning Inc.
All rights reserved. No part of this publication may be reproduced, stored in a retrieval system, or transmitted in any form or by any means, electronic, mechanical, photocopying, recording, or otherwise, without the prior written permission of the publisher.

Library of Congress Control Number: 2025937844

ISBN 978-1-5105-8265-1 (hardcover)
ISBN 978-1-5105-8266-8 (static multi-user eBook)
ISBN 978-1-5105-8268-2 (interactive multi-user eBook)

Printed in Fargo, North Dakota, in the United States of America
1 2 3 4 5 6 7 8 9 0 29 28 27 26 25

062025
110824

Project Coordinator: Heather Kissock
Designer: Terry Paulhus
Layout: Jean Faye Rodriguez

The publisher has made every reasonable effort to trace ownership and to obtain permission to use copyright material. The publisher would be pleased to have any errors or omissions brought to its attention so that they may be corrected in subsequent printings. Some visual elements in this title may have been generated using AI. While we strive for accuracy in all aspects of our products, we cannot guarantee that the elements depicted in these images are accurate. The publisher acknowledges Getty Images, Alamy, and Shutterstock as the primary image suppliers for this title. If you have any inquiries about these images or would like to provide any feedback, please reach out to us at feedback@openlightbox.com

All of the Internet URLs and Google Maps links given in the interactive eBook were valid at the time of publication. However, due to the dynamic nature of the Internet, some addresses may have changed, or sites may have ceased to exist since publication. While the author and publisher regret any inconvenience this may cause readers, no responsibility for any such changes can be accepted by either the author or the publisher.